BLACK

BLACK

❧

George Elliott Clarke

POLESTAR
An Imprint of Raincoast Books

Copyright © 2006 by George Elliott Clarke
All photographs © by the photographers. See page 148 for full details.

The moral right of the author has been asserted.

First Printing, MMVI

Raincoast Books gratefully acknowledges the ongoing support of the Canada Council for the Arts, the British Columbia Arts Council and the Government of Canada through the Book Publishing Industry Development Program (BPIDP).

Edited by Silas White.
Cover and interior design by Teresa Bubela.
Author photograph by Le Roi Ray.

Library and Archives Canada

Clarke, George Elliott, 1960-
    Black / George Elliott Clarke.
Poems.
ISBN 10 1-55192-903-1
ISBN 13 978-1-55192-903-3
    I. Title.
PS8555.L3748B53 2006   C811'.54   C2005-905459-X

Raincoast Books   *In the United States:*
9050 Shaughnessy Street   Publishers Group West
Vancouver, British Columbia   1700 Fourth Street
Canada V6P 6E5   Berkeley, California
www.raincoast.com   94710

Printed in Canada by Houghton-Boston.

10 9 8 7 6 5 4 3 2 1

BLACK *Power*

Je suis noire, si noire qu'on y voit plus clair.
— CALIXTHE BEYALA

These poems are *black*, deviant, defiant. Inked in the shadow of *Blue* (2001), they also echo The Great Republic's gregarious rages.

True: I am African-Canadian. My roots go back two centuries in Nova Scotia; and, before that, to the U.S. So I am also African-American, *proudly*. But my "belonging" carries an asterisk, one shaped like a — ragged — maple leaf.

A sort-of African-American and a so-so English-Canadian, I read Irving Layton through the lens of Jean Toomer — without jive, without apology. The blackness of my English be that of ice.

GEORGE ELLIOTT CLARKE (X. STATES)

TORONTO, ONTARIO

Nisan VI

BLACK *Market*

and I know how various yet unchanging
Blackness is ...

— CAROLYN M. RODGERS

BLACK *Lung*

As to black, only the mentally troubled are usually fascinated by it.
— FABER BIRREN

George & Rue: Coda

I — January 7, 1949

Near midnight, Rufus slammed the hammer
Down, down — bam! — into Burgundy's head —

Like a bullet bashing the skull.
The night heard a man halloo, "Oh!"

At that stabbing noise, George whipped around.
The hurt cab bled as black as a hearse.

The moon that night: a white man's face.
Winds flickered black, slick, in the pines.

When Georgie sidled down the hill, glidin
Back to the car, Br'er Rudy already had

Burgundy's wallet tugged out his pocket.
Blood hugged Rue's body, snuggled up

His face. Giorgio shoved Burgundy aside,
So he could fist cash, watch, rosary, coins.

Later, George stove the taxi, a cadaver
Fluffed in the trunk, in Fredericton's snow,

And slinked off, whistling, to drink, drink, drink.
Snow cleansed everything, but memory.

The taxicab leaked a smoke-trail of blood.
Just because.

Georgie weren't chilled; he waltzed back where
Rue be guzzlin blackberry wine in brand-new clothes.

Rue ain't feel nothin bad or wrong or upset.
A white man was dead, yes; but they had booze and cash.

II — Trials & Convictions

Geo: Everyone says
     The noose is soon.

Rue: What they mean is,
     Life's meaning's gone.

Geo: After I die, let my words be rain, grass:
I don't mind, in April, in Three Mile Plains.

Rue: Gravediggers got job security,
And murderers got no reason to be jealous.

Justice: It will be a crisply, British-accented lynching.
To exterminate two germs.

Narrator: The hanging? Will be very disgusting.
Of two pterodactyls. Very disgusting.

The Edvard Munch moon screams like Pound
In night's icebox, while Van Gogh stars go mad.

III — The Hangings

The gallows is carpentered so passionately,
Love itself seems engrained in the pine.

The pale, soft, easily worked pine
Transforms the gallows into a guillotine.

The two young Negro men, unhinged,
Swing lazily to a bluegrass, Dixieland tune.

A murmur of light, eh?
Then stars expire in dew.

That repugnant civil servant, the hangman,
After this Sadean idyll, will cultivate brambles.

10,000 mad dogs bay and wolf-whistle
The outfoxed boys' falls.

The clangour of two hangings:
Those dangling feet, pealing.

Letter to a Young Poet

Go ahead and compose a poem on *Love*:
You'll poison it with the poetry —
Sly darkness without any sweetness.
See, the poet's body whelps carrion-insects,
Vomits some worms, some ants, some wasps, some bees —
Things malevolent and marvellous at once,
Their horrifically mixed-up mouths chewing,
Ripping, devastating, your heart.
Poetry eats its lovers alive.

You could get your throat slashed for this —
This ominous obsession.

But you have no shame:
No, you have the face of a crushed horse,
And capering therein a million maggots
Usurping every prickle of light.

Language

for Wendy "Motion" Braithwaite

I hate this language that *Hate* dictates to me.
It gusts the tang and bray of a savage civilization —
Violent words violently arrived at.

Balderdash and *braggadocio*: what English is —
Squabbling cabals in Bibles and newspapers —
A tongue that cannibalizes all other tongues.

Speculate on the words still bottled blackly
In placid ink —
Fear what may leap from that *Innocence* ...

2

This homely poem's a queer nigger rig,
A botch of art in slovenly English,
Bad grammar, bad everything;
It cannot perform ethically.
It even fucks up Black English badly:
The metre harries, but the words refuse to fit.

3

for Evelyn Shockley

That bang, blackening, of English syllables
In my black-black mouth hurts,
Them syllables hurt,
So I can only vomit up speech —
Half-digested English —
Soiling it with virulent Negro stomach juices.
Ma voice ain't *classique!*

4

Grammar is pollution, some poison in my lungs,
So what emerges from my mouth — spit, phlegm —
Looks tubercular.

My lopsided tongue spoils Her Majesty's English.
The jawbreaker words wad my mouth with blood,
Even busted teeth.

I spit out *vers* — ruddy larvae, red writhing worms —
Like a TB victim hawking scarlet phlegm into a sink.

5

A "herring-choker" Negro with a breath of brine,
I gabble a *garrote* argot, guttural, by rote,
A wanton lingo, taunted and tainted by wine,
A feinting *langue* haunted by each slave boat.

My black, "Bluenose" brogue smacks lips and ears
When I bite the bitter grapes of Creole verse —
Or gripe and blab like a Protestant pope
So rum-pungent Africa mutes perfumed Europe.

Of Black English, or Pig Iron Latin

for Kaie Kellough

My brain were brass, fucked, alloyed
By alliteration. It were dazzlingly dull
For a nigger, niggling with English,
Haggling o'er some moping poem,
Cut from a second-hand grammar,
Rhyming Oxonian *et* Negronian.
        Zounds! My lyrics was tin-plate,
Not steel-sheet, some gift of gabble,
Une blague, maybe glib bilge.
Oui? What was needed were, was —
After some hectic loss of respect —
Higher quality coal — or iron — or gold …

(A tinny Walcott, I would like, I'd like,
Black English to sound more like tempered steel.)

Spoken Word

My imperfect pitch is pitch,
mingling woodpile (niggerish)

and woodwind (ebony)?
Sheeeit, motherfucker, all you do's

invent stray, pungent lyrics,
callous as *jacquerie*, violent

as addled presidents,
to clap boisterousness into poetry,

to collide words together.
Go, scratch poems in frost,

daub poems in sweat.
Ain't Shakespeare a broke-ass tongue,

mixing pig's breath of sulphur
with horse's breath of sugar,

some unpronounceable English trash —
rancid, acidic, rash? Balderdash!

Topaz, patois poets —
why use somebody else's language

badly,
baldly?

Rather, labour
over Braille.

IV. i

for H. Nigel Thomas

Can I report these repercussions?
A bloody English, carved from concussions
and cusses —
cutlassed asses and atlases —
grammar scummed far, so far, off an Oxford
or Webster disciplinary.
There's the *priminery*:
What else — meet — can a poet, Black, afford?

I tried to lift an entire ocean into literature —
the slaver's Atlantic, yes, Africa's sepulchre.
It were easy, so easy, I thought:
I just chanted —
disenchanted —
a lot — with my lot.

But to lean forward was, I learned,
to study the *crepuscolari* poets, not the pale ones,
who disappear, jaded,
falling from anthologies,
flaming out as if fevered,
their words dissolving into white voids.
I had to sing — or wring out — *black* noise:
dat hubbub and hurly-burly of Halifax pubs,
girly, boyo, all *dat* hurdy-gurdy gabble,
all *dat* bumpy, lumpy, frumpy speech!

Oui, eh?

IV. ii

for Andrea Thompson

The blasphemy of our Negro pagan crying
Gainst Euro Lit's deathly white pages
Be a rude caricature of eloquence.
Admit it: Our vocabulary come from provincial
Flippancy; our tongues tipple English gone sour.
We be so much ill-lettered than them *Tarzan* fops,
Or them executed, ice-eyed existentialists.
We be Zombies outmoded, not *des tontons macoutes.*

So let them supercilious Caucasian critics
Praise — slavishly — our "exuberant, sing-song
Poetry," our "sure-good-jive," our "Rap rhymes,"
Our "big smiles," our big fun with "big words."

This be the repercussions of black voice —
To be dark ivy vying against marble tombs.

IV. iii

for Clifton Joseph

Black is black and black and black
Black is a *nègre* nigger, a *negrita* nigger, a *schwartz* nigger
Black is mulatto, sambo, negro, quadroon, octoroon
Black is Africa, darkest Africa, as photographed by Leni Riefenstahl
Black is the best Scotch, the best chocolates, the best sex
Black is lilies, isles of lilies, and their gold, trumpeting perfume
Black is purple prose, blue movies, red flags
Black is white turned inside out until it shows its true colours
Black is Bessie Smith's black bottom you are invited, politely, to kiss
Black is Wynton Marsalis trying desperately to equal Miles Davis
Black is what "the definition of is *is*"
Black is fiascoes of perversion after failures of imagination
Black is the critical neglect of [insert name of favourite writer here]
Black is a listing in the Montréal phone book
Black is black *Parker* ink in a *Hauser* black metal fountain pen ejaculating words
Black is almost 5h with a bottle of *Bença* Brazilian rum behind you
          and a bottle of *TUMS* before you
Black is glass splinters in your sphincter
Black is Othello, Aaron the Moor, Caliban, and Falstaff
Black is the English Queen of Canada lisping Pig Latin in Paris, Ontario
Black is the highest standard, highest calibre, of white
Black is roses turned to sorrow
Black is confusing Carole Laure with Laure Sainclair
Black is puritanical sex, which is good, and depraved sex, which is very good
Black is maple brass coffee iron mahogany copper cocoa bronze ebony
          chocolate

Black is Henry Dumas, Conrad Kent Rivers, Robert Hayden, and
Wanda Coleman
Black is Grit-commissioned sin and Tory-committed crime
Black is *Love's Labours Lost, Measure for Measure*, after *Much Ado About Nothing*
Black is your ass, your bowels, your morals
Black is your love of mere words
Black is the future of *Blue*
Black is *Whylah Falls, Beatrice Chancy, Execution Poems*, and *Black* —
Choirs of light.

BLACK *Ink*

J'ai le style noir du vautour.
— JOVETTE MARCHESSAULT

Self-plagiarism is style.
— ALFRED HITCHCOCK

Beginning

circa 1975

A pen chisels its way cross paper
And all my thoughts scrape out.

Skinny, lanky, buck-toothed, four-eyed bookworm:
I write the bottle dry.

Sing rickety, groggily,
Blues scrawled with troubled pencils.

Clarinets point skyward like dandelions.
Wine gets illegally drunk.

Gypsy gals hum, "Peace, Order, Good Government":
Dreaming marks the distance twixt dark and dawn.

Verse is opera, history a museum.
Let pages swim with cusses.

What will poets say
When my music's gone at last?

Poetry: 1/7/75—1/7/05

> *Should I make my way out of my home in the woods?*
> — BERNIE TAUPIN

I — Standards

Each poem perishes and replenishes,
Line by line.

Even if you copy poets
Smashed to smithereens

By iambs
(or "I am's"),

Note that the truest black poet
Is a nappy-headed Dadaist —

If the poem is in fine form
(No matter how frail),

Tattling the *Truth*,
Outtalking critics.

The good poem stabs like a dagger now,
Explodes later like a grenade.

II — The Canon

Chaucer's guffaws discharge baroque ferocity.
Scornful parody is Pound's Torquemada art.

Whitman champions matter-of-fact hoopla.
Plath quills sado-maso, melodramatic jitters.

Henry Dumas crows the gravelly authentic.
Robert Hayden composes cozy razzmatazz.

Abrasive jests define mod, clerical Eliot.
Gothic Milton thunders classical damnations.

Hopkins prays with congested hyperbole.
Ginsberg howls self-vauntingly robust.

Dr. Donne heads up a raunchy church.
Poe, drunk, radiates macabre intensity.

Baudelaire's putrid vivacity audaciously
Answers Rimbaud's helter-skelter images.

Blake drafts a do-it-yourself religion
Echoing Li Po's angelic, moonlit songs.

Thomas's madcap medievality
Prompts Dylan's bellicose folksiness.

Jean Toomer stages fermented, Old South theatre,
Accented by Burns's 100-proof, demented Scotch.

Irving Layton unfurls caustic tongue-lashings,
But Alden Nowlan oozes backwoods swank.

Walcott's Nobel, indelible excellence
Flouts Shakespeare's deadpan majesty.

III — *Principles*

My own *gaucherie* and rectitude
Result from sparkling thievery.

My cranky pantomimes,
My blackface prettifications

Of "masters and mistresses,"
Expose my uppity stealing.

Like a real poet,
I am unfaithful, disloyal, treasonous.

Lit'ry, but bumptious,
I disputes da bullwhip.

A black man cannot hide —
Eh? — in the page's white skin.

When you think of my ink,
Or meditate on a page,

Pay attention to the blackness,
Its rich darkness.

Ink and voice — the liqueurs of the savage —
Ignite the very fire of freedom.

Imagine this ink is flame
Burning the page as you read.

This voice, my very own,
Be a saxophone disrupting sirens.

My nervous, excited poetics
Be quite shaky with verbs.

IV — Confessions

This pen I use to break open my thoughts
Issues psychological blues.

No matter how comically meticulous,
My canvas is the blues.

All true songs acknowledge *Pain*,
But *Love* is everything.

My truest poems are unforgettably true —
Like skillful executioners.

I compromise *Wrong* and *Right*
Because every good song is ambivalent.

No matter where you are,
You are here with me.

Together, we have chosen this ending.
There is never enough time for words.

À *Alexander Pushkin*

à la manière de Paul Zemokhol

I

As smooth and as supple as ink,
My voice sails this foaming paper

To your unknowable shores,
Where you are living, secretly.

I smuggle my voice into this thin craft,
As fragile as radio transmissions.

Is it clear?
Are you awake to its nuances, its codes?

I give you my hand — cursive, discursive,
Wafting across this page as white as bone

And as soft as a tongue.
I mean, my hand is a tongue —

Just as this page is a spine —
If my words are sound.

II

Your iodine-brown skin, minutely ebony,
Obstinately citric, like stunning oranges,

Holds blood weighed — like gold — in ounces.
Its ritzy history issues as light spraying from a projector.

Black and brown folk finesse bliss from blues,
So Russia melted under your searing comedy, your hot tragedy.

You knew there's no merriment in a monastery,
No nitty-gritty, deep-down *Love*.

All your czars fell drunk, all your saints got fucked,
All your Romantic heroes fought losing duels.

Listen: Negro God set Eden in Africa,
And coloured Adam and Eve as black as Heaven

Praised by all those pale, waning stars.
Poet, it's our duty to astonish the sun and stun the moon.

À Edgar Mittelhölzer

à la manière de Sonnet L'Abbé

I

Your writing writhes;
Your words flood out, bloody.

Jet-black ink jets across the pure, pale page:
A delicious rape, eh? Caliban tupping Miranda.

The white whore whelps a black child: *Poetry.*
But it's not *Britannia*'s, it's yours.

Coloured poet, black man with white skin,
Is it best to be decisively black, or half-evil but all-white?

How do you get to write like a poet
Where mothers' screams multiply like roaches?

The wound of *History* spews *Poetry*'s blood:
Spirituals and proverbs, Blues and sermons, Gospel and newspapers.

The English poets tut-tut; the Yankee poets yap.
But the true Negro poet sings and drums and cries.

II

An Afro and Cathay Guyana, a Hindu Guyana,
Inspires *Literature* wanton with miscegenation,

That vague ague plaguing everything.
The rat — your king — was also your crop.

Your capital, Georgetown, hosts a harlot dubbed "Parliament":
She talks too much and seats many members.

Guyana is a fen of cock — and blood — suckers!
Ain't blood-and-guts destruction just so Guyanese?

III

Your laurels: thorns, a decrepit glory.
The grand poets get crowned with magnolia.

Cheshire cat, smiling through crocodile tears,
You meted out *Beauty* like meat: dead meat.

IV

You composed chamber opera from chamber pots.
You were like a dissertation best used as a faggot.

You died breathlessly,
A lantern of fire.*

Mittel=middle; *hölzer*=woodworker:
You died like a log in the middle of a fireplace.

When I see you in your shroud of fire,
I see Tom Thomson, fainting, in an acre of water,

A fishing hook in his throat, in Algoma.
A dirty laugh huffing up.

You were blazing like a heat wave in August.
Your flames splintered you like a mirror.

We'll mix your cold ashes with the earth until,
Crumbly, slushy, you're fresh India ink —

A black flag of ink
Proclaiming anarchy — or piracy — in a white desert.

Your ashen heart reveals this ashen prophecy:
All ex-colonial speakers of English be liars.

* *Mittelhölzer (1909–65) committed suicide by setting himself alight.*

À Arthur Nortje

*Nay, if there be no remedy for it, but that you will needs buy and sell men and
women like beasts, we shall have all the world breed brown and white bastard.*
— MEASURE FOR MEASURE

Such golden, muddy lees: your poetics —
That sulphurous lava —
Standard for mixed-race mix-ups, snafus,
Who distill piss-yellow acid from brown sugar:

Your vernacular sops and oozes black ink,
The colour of drool out a smashed mouth,
Stammering, dyeing all those white grammars,
Blotting the air.

Your genealogy parses *apartheid* holocaust —
The melting flesh around the smoking brand,
The icy feel of chains like intimate jewellery ...

From *gulags* of oblivion and limbo, you flit,
Tan vampire, to suck white and black teats,
To bleed South Africa and give Canada ebola.

Au Tombeau de Pound (II)

Those gardens of the honest great
Never, ever disintegrate.
Though green cemeteries languish
In *Decay*, ingenious *Anguish* —
Spiritual fount of *Art* — vaults
Past moldered bone and marble faults
To become ageless *craquelure* —
A *disjecta membra* sinecure —
Piecing as one each masterpiece
With lustrous seams, gold without cease,
So that its memory is *Song* —
Lyrical as light — and as strong.

The *chiaroscuro* of your script
Plies sunned ivy to dismal crypt,
And now among your deathless words
Creep schooled liars and skirling lizards.
In this Eden, where you lie dead,
Blast forth flowers, beautiful, blood-red,
Along with light, more and more light,
Defined by shadow, defied by night.
In this isled, hot, cypress space,
I still take umbrage and solace,
In your flaming poems, and their shade,
Cantos sung in the key of Sade.

V. i

1

Hate Pound vomits,
Sly Yeats omits.

2

Not a man, but a thundercloud.
Lay him bare: you'll harvest lightning.

3

I have read my Pound.
It was not "child's play."
In fact, I can say
I feel still the wound.

Not just *The Cantos*
Disgust and dismay,
But also *Cathay*
And *A Lume Spento.*

Listen: his lies hiss
Mussolini's lines.
But deaf *Art* declines
His death in Venice.

V. ii

à Cimitero, Venezia

A lizard skitters among the toppled stones
stoppling this sinking — if Serene — Republic–
propped upon mudbanks and *guano*,
where Othello did the State black service
and spit himself upon his sword,
and Pound came *pianissimo* to die —
after pusillanimous ravings in a cage.
A gurgling disaster — like his — shines all around.
      Here cypresses re-enact hanged Shylocks,
the vines strangle like piano wire;
the squalid, venomous sea induces
an undulant, rainbow-oily dissolve
sapping, undermining, isled headstones,
and softening Pound's *Duce*-rigid bones,
so that once-ivory temple of lyric
flounders upon his sewer politics.
      The Adriatic silvers stained marble;
lightning whitewashes rotting cathedrals;
but *Poetry*'s caustic light unmasks
that Rio Tera dei Assassini partisan,
whose crabby shadow scuttles this page,
bullying, shaming, sullying every line.

Wintering

A whole shelf of books on Pound:
The Inferno in translation.

The car dons its winter coat of white —
Like black people, slipping past slaughter,

Slavery. Camouflage is the turncoat's
Treason. What are you against

But can't say?
                      We are against
Each other in bed, in love, the snow

Tilting the earth, cantilevering the sky.
The coffee smells like paper, burning.

The slippery slaves bear a crust of white,
Surging into Canada, its chilly faces,

As lunatic as pale Pound in his *plein-air* cage,
Looming, like Pisa's tower, against our type.

Sermon on J.W. Doull's Used Books Store

La poésie est un art utile.
— PIERRE ELLIOTT TRUDEAU

Shakespeare and Milton bump against
        Demimondaines like Longfellow,
Or faint luminaries like McKuen, but
        Avoid anonymous, dead stars —
Discards, pitilessly banished to bins
        (Ignorant that professors praised
Their lines to judgmental undergrads,
        Who would not forsake French kisses,
Or Irish ale, to entrench a poet's words
        In *Lust*-capped, *Lust*-capacious skulls.)

Discounted, musty, some who anguish
        Over lines must languish in mildew
Graves until some light-summoning poet
        Plucks them from rust obscurity.

BLACK *Earth*

Black is beautiful.

— 1960S AFRICAN-AMERICAN MAXIM

Towards a Geography of Three Mile Plains, N.S.

Times are bad and the poet is broke,
but around him is that permanent world of Beauty ...
— JAMES WILHELM

Remember the well and its water encrusted by ice
And rusted by piss, the bull that stank as rankly as a bull,
And your Bible's leather binding, black, that seemed to bleed.
The pear tree was made for lightning strikes (three strikes),
While the Ten Commandments ordained the saintly stoning
Of windows in abandoned, dead-minister-owned houses,
Whose forgotten pianos sprouted icky, sickening weeds.
Up Green Street, in gold-leaf dusks, two copper-coloured
Cowboys could saunter, leading miniature, tan ponies
Into the gold sunflower sun coppering their faces. Native,
They were anthropologically black, psychologically black,
Despite a white war-bride-mama ex-"De Ol' Country."
The apples shaken from trees were gangrenous blossoms
Showering upon burial plots blurring into potato patch.
The hay you tumbled in, covered with kisses, was ripe
For recumbent, blonde-gal cousins to be so seductive in,
With hickory-scented hair and hickory-smoked breasts,
Until spasms, *passim.* Some lover'd exclaim, "Like it?
Lick it!" Harmonicas harmonized night and wind, lilies
And root beer, while the train, smokingly bitchy, bluesy,
And restless, went huffing past ponds and chicken coops
And the sewage lagoon (a tanner's horse tethered nearby).
While crickets chimed accord, you set bulrushes alight,
Ached to unscramble poems from brambles and kinky ink,

Beside railroad tracks where lovers wallowed, juicy, using
Mosquitoes, thorns, gravel, for temporary underwear,
And screwed sloppily, even with bites of all sorts digging
Into sweet flesh, that was tan or pale or black, equalized.
Then it was you down there in the funk and honey slime,
The slippery night uncoiling oily between your soiled thighs
Where the mosquitoes had been crushed, and a girl's hand,
First Caucasian, French-speaking, next Negro and English,
Was communicating her, your, lust with illicit liqueurs
And sugary wine mixed with racial theories you exploded.
Brit professors and cracker cops harrumphed, in perfect
Sneering grammar, again and again, "You have NO history."
True: *our* Stonehenge was just a bunch of dominoes
Stood on one end — a penurious gambler's last stand …

VI. i

for Walter M. Borden, C.M.

The Imperial Rose Garden and its plush jungle flora
        Imitate what Sappho loved — this red, blushed
Majesty, cascading dastardly in patchwork patterns
        That mirror triangulated, assassins' gunfire.
Magenta, scarlet, fragile pink, *noir*, and white,
        The roses mass perplexingly complex in tinge —
Like a political party of Machiavellian intent.
        But forget policy! Enjoy *rouge*-gorgeous air,
Smelling also of perfumed decay like a bordello,
        That stench of bedsheets after coitus
(Rank sweat and drool, ointments and condiments),
        Amid dog hair strewn like strychnine to scare off
Impressionable deer, and the light sluicing down
        Like loose juice, a stew of drenching spunk.
Jewels of insects glitter amid the pulp and juice
        Of russet pears, sapped, crushed, but teeming
Also with maggots as fierce as asps. Nearby, bees
        Burrow into the fragrant, pouting vaginas
Of impious flowers, dousing themselves with nectar —
        Delicious, sopping — until they resemble
Lavishly lolling lovers, busy with *queynte*-moistened
        Faces. Leave them and go down the plank walk
Among the elephant grass (or Norfolk reed) to spy
        The dead railroad bridge — all rusted iron and

Rotting wood, a Canuck Stonehenge, a paean
  To Confederation's steady decay. Look! A gang
Of crows parliaments the telephone lines. They are
  Like honourable members nodding stolidly
At each other, "ahem"-ing and "amen"-ing about
  Their ingenious and eternal pension plans.
The sky is sapphire broken by grey-white shards,
  But the ground stinks of dying apples, berries,
Smelling much like March and April with their vernal
  Muck. A mosquito zeroes in among shadowy,
Gold-streaked, man-tall, zebra grass clusters, while I'm
  Watching bulrushes salute overbearing,
Sky-fucking trees such as the *Populus Caroliniana*
  (or Carolina Poplar), which looks nine-storeys
High, at least four-feet thick, and now, where this ink
  Is smudged, that reckless mosquito lies wrecked.

I pass a pond, no fresher than it was three years ago
        (Unlike the fresh ejaculation of a line),
Mid-September, in Annapolis Royal's Historic Gardens.
        Hear the *fizz* of the mini waterfall — as quiet
As lethal flowers that have no scent. Here is a new
        Dragonfly, navigating purple-blue among
Green-and-gold lily pads and lofty, saw-grass spears.
        Time is aging, time is aging, and is ageless,
While tree limbs rake upward like algebraic formula,
        Composing a jazz of randomness — just like
Our never-finished lines, leaping from direction
        To direction: a *vers libre* architecture.
Again, now, the reek of rot under a thrusting tree —
        The scraggly, straggling, bedraggled arches
Of a flouncing, hydra-headed tree. The sun mirrors it,
        Launching arrows of light, lancing, almost,
The obdurate, darkening clouds, as it surrenders
        To the puny daggers of incensed mosquitoes,
Jabbing us like pens jab paper, pricking, pricking,
        Until ink runs like blood.

The poet is, the poet is,
        A gardener in a graveyard.

Africadian Experience

for Frederick Ward

To howl in the night because of smoked rum wounding the heart;
To be so stubbornly crooked, your alphabet develops rickets;
To check into the Sally Ann — and come out brain-dead, but spiffy;
To smell the sewer anger of politicians washed up by dirty votes;
To feel your skin burning under vampire kisses meant for someone else;
To trash the ballyhooed verses of the original, A-1, Africville poets;
To carry the Atlantic into Montreal in epic suitcases with Harlem accents;
To segregate black and white bones at the behest of discriminating worms;
To mix voodoo alcohol and explosive loneliness in unsafe bars;
To case the Louvre with raw, North Preston gluttony in your eyes;
To let vitamin deficiencies cripple beauty queens in their beds;
To dream of Halifax and its collapsing houses of 1917
       (Blizzard and fire in ten thousand living rooms in one day);
To stagger a dirt road that leads to an exploded piano and bad sermons;
To plumb a well that taps rice wine springing up from China;
To okay the miracle of a split length of wood supporting a clothesline;
To cakewalk into prison as if you were parading into Heaven;
To recognize *Beauty* when you see it and to not be afraid.

Land

for Olive Senior

       Compared to the sky, it is nullity —
Nothing is built on it but history.
But light saturates its pastures, kindling gold,
And winter idles there, ladling on ice,
And April purls, stinking and muck-sodden,
And summer whelps weeds, snakes, wasps, and sunflowers,
And October showers down dead stars and leaves,
       And maybe a poet hunches on a tree stump,
Scribbling about faceless ancestors gone
Underground, but whose faces carry on
In his vivid, vivaciously ruined, own,
And suspecting he is rooted, he feels
It is because he can see — treed — new stars.

À St. Matthias

for Oni Joseph

Robert Sandiford snaps my colourized photo
at grey-stone St. Matthias Anglican Church

just outside sea-bleached Bridgetown, Barbados.
Whimsically, we stopped here because Austin C.

Clarke was a boy here. The sun's now as white
as the stones where Bro' Austin worshipped

an Anglo-Saxon Christ, his stiff upper lip never
trembling when the spear and whips struck.

And there's the sapphire sea, a lowered sky,
blue jewellery, sparking mid dark-green trees,

and the sea churns white among the grey stones,
and the Parliament is a whited sepulchre

at the slave auction site where it now sits,
while the Atlantic crows at blanching sand,

And then Robert's auto dies, forcing us to walk,
cursing, blaspheming, in Austin's footsteps.

À Bellagio

Should I write this or not —
A line about "insects disrespecting my ankles"?
Lizards — like switchblades — pocket themselves,
diving in slithery cracks —
like minor poets among their pentameters.
The sun glints off insects disrespecting my ankles,
while my shadow, elongating across syllables
and pebbles, blanks out this page.
Lizards drizzle over stones.

     A crimson tractor, chortling, ferries
nothing that can be guessed at.
First, it's obscured by a large tree;
but, it's red again as it returns to view,
hauling what looks like moss,
but isn't. It's just words.

     Now in the fishing village next door —
a man on a boat squints,
visors his eyes to study me like a critic.
I am, I guess, strange, foreign, Negro,
and given to criminal, dithyrambic obsessions.

     Now a dog squawks at unconcerned ducks,
until a man bawls *Basta!*
and it stops.

And its master, sprawling at his table under grapes and grape leaves,
Slices bologna for his animal.

  Leaves shine like seashells in the dusking sunlight.
A bee divagates among flowers.
(If only I had a botanist's exact eye,
and could accent every florid scent with Latin!)

  Clambering the cliffy hillside, I remember
Hannibal ranging, punitive, through these Alps,
in Pyrrhic triumph,
then Mussolini falling, a bulleted cadaver,
his black fedora flying.

  Eyeing such plenitude, the poem overflows,
the words coming and coming and coming …

À *Bellagio (II)*

Now I must say goodbye olive trees,
goodbye rosemary, goodbye *pasticceria*,
goodbye *gelateria*, goodbye white-black butterfly
with the brown stripe, goodbye Villa Serbelloni —
with crooked doors and crack-radiant paintings,
goodbye to that book of Chinese characters
with its watercolour plates shimmering
green plants and yellow or pink flowers,
ciao to all the extraordinary women,
and goodbye *Campari*, gin, and vermouth,
goodbye to *grappa* & *negroni* & *limoncello*,
goodbye to the blistering roses,
goodbye to the great books, the greatest books,
and goodbye to that black scorpion.

April Blizzard, Kingston to Gananoque

An opaque storm avalanches from April clarity,
volleys ivory squalls against windshields,
so the freeway blanks out whitely, darkly,
under an instant *tsunami* of snow.

Drivers panic, vehicles jackknife;
travellers spiral and gyre like Icarus,
Then vapourize horribly in fire and snow —
like a glacier struck suddenly by lava.

Nisan

for Lorena Gale

1

Delinquent, deliquescent snow.

Snarl of rain in the branches.

Pale light ploughing the fields.

2

Blossoms of snow on the leafless peach trees:
This chill cuts greenly, nixing November's
Sepia cold. Numbingly new snow arcs,
Spiking — sparking — down, spurring recharged grass
To thrust upwards, preening. Next, this April
Scuds down rain, polishing pearly lenses
Of water in fields: Could such charged, endless
Churn even scour away Parliament's filth?

Regard: Little rills slur the frothed river,
Aluminum-luminate, numinous,
Bright as tinny, sitcom laughter, drowning
Out every serious thing. Then, lightning
Punches down through clouds, while rain's lush push,
Rush, and gush, a crushing inundation,
Flushes out snow, but foundations first flowers.

La Vérité à Ottawa

April came thundering-and-lightning in, with snow,
And icy rain drapes, cascades of cold wet,
And sodden chrysanthemums out of nowhere,
And the shock of purple-and-white crocus daubing
The southeast slope of Parliament Hill, by the canal,
And then the surge of sun, lemony, cantankerous, warm,
But still also sprays and squalls of recalcitrant snow,
So that the canal swelled and seethed with gobs of ice
And brimmed, heavy with that seashell-shade weight,
Pouring through the Rideau Locks and into the Ottawa
River — like tons of white-and-grey-blue salmon,
Reversing themselves.

Leaving Afro-Arab-Asian-Italian Lowertown —
The Coloured *arrondissement* of Ottawa — then crossing
The Eddy Street Bridge, you'd see, on your left,
The frothing falls of the E.B. Eddy factory, the clean
White energy of the water charging into channels
To electrify turbines and generators, with the Peace
Tower behind you, in the rear-view mirror, thrusting,
Marvellously erect — despite all the eunuchs droning
In its bowels.

Here you refluxed an acidic love that seeped
Into all the sutures and silences of the marriage
And corrupted it, while Arctic cold axed your face,
And the spindly trees before the Château Laurier
Put on stalactites and daggers.

      Next came the bitterness of tabloids, Mulroney's
Tories trashing the treasury, the upper-class defecating
Their taxes on the lower orders — the rest of us. There was
The skirl of leaves in autumn and the skitter of whores' heels
In the always summery Byward Market,
And, also, the molten memory of failure —

      A love that was Druid and lurid and Gothic,
So befitting Ottawa, city of fits and paralysis,
Where nothing could save me from lonesome
Strutting along Parliament Hill and gutting
An original — virginal — marriage with aboriginal lust
For an Afro-Sino Jamaican, fluent in French and English,
Equally official under the Constitution,
While ice-galled winds scalded — facetious — my face.

La Vérité à Ottawa (II)

The National Library dispensed no relief
Despite its voluptuous, frosted glass reliefs
Of Greco-Roman nymphs depicting
Trans-Atlantic, Caucasian cleavage.

    No, there was no relief in that Stalinist edifice,
That slate-smooth, white-grey *bibliothèque*,
That sloughed off, bureaucratically,
Artwork positioned to soften its entrance —
The *Secret Bench of Knowledge*, a sculpture
Of a boy and a girl sharing an apple on a park bench,
Where I had scrawled in the wax bronze,
"Here we'll
edge close
to happiness."

    No, there was, for me, no relief
From wanting another woman, not my then-wife,
To narrow my bed.

    After wanton, surreptitious, Platonic strolls,
Along the dusk'd canal, strangers egging us on,
Gushing, "She's beautiful! She's beautiful!"
Or editorializing, unasked,
"You make such a cinematic couple,"
She'd smile incisors, glistening,
While I pocketed my ring-fingered left hand,
To feign unadulterated innocence.

Later, while whores guffawed and growled
Outside my ground-floor apartment window *au marché*,
I suffered vicious, viscous visions
Of that Bible-toting tease, that hymn-singing quim,
That wriggle of a woman in a squiggle of a dress,
Her crucifix jittering between her breasts,
Their scented *émail* of baby powder and sweat,
Then imagine her slender waist (not want not)
Juicing under praying kisses, slobbered valentines,
Our bodies configured in Pythagorean obscenities.

    Ah! My dreams — those rain-clouded sunflowers —
Drooped to a sewer,
Cos I wilted, unwilling to maul a gilt Gioconda,
A unique queen, Aprilicious,
To bid red wine issue us to malicious delicacies,
My *prima facie* lust slutting her *prima donna* looks,
With nothing on but Sade's sinuous voice
Insinuating there's no sensation *sans* sin,
While I hauled my mad self up to *ma donna*'s hilt.

    Love? I know I've here wounded the word.
If I could compose a real sincere poetry —
Of unexcelled lyric quality,
I mean, if I could be as frank as Anne Frank ...
But ink papers over tears even as it tears paper.

Damn it! Damn it! Damn it!
The truth is,
Had I been unflinchingly, laughingly arrogant,
Disdainful of her sanctimonious heart,
Dismissive of her acrimonious tongue,
Disrespectful to her parsimonious flesh,
Her belligerent elegance, as spiteful as fire,
Had I melted down, in *sotto voce* soldering,
That iron-haired, copper-skinned, tin-hearted,
        leaden-voiced saint,
Had her high heels teetered to low morals,
Had we, in effect, come crotch-to-crotch
In a lush organ grinding of plush organs,
I'd not be authoring this moping poem,
This elegy for lacustrine blackness,
While my dissolute lust, my blue cryings,
Pucker my lips into a dismal clarinet …

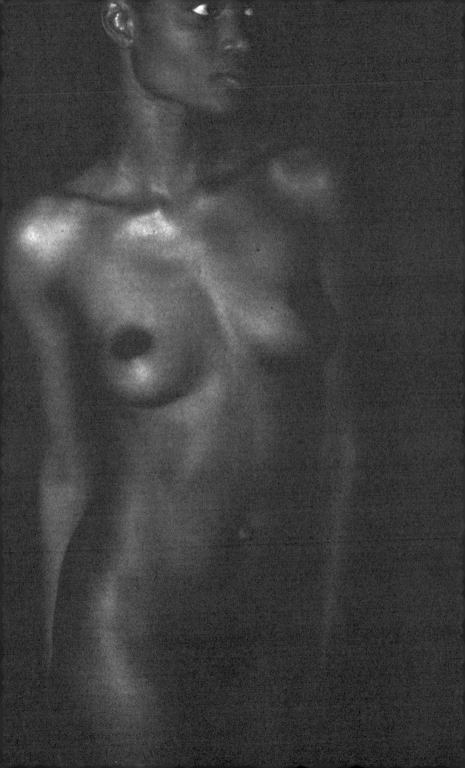

BLACK *Eye*

Blackness was one of the conditions of beauty.

— FRANK YERBY

VII

à la manière de Robert Edison Sandiford

You who are insolent as anatomically-correct dolls,
You, with your bilingual faces and black-leather *nichons*,
you who shout, "*Boulot, métro, sodo!*" in that order,
you who are all show *devants* and all *chauds derrières*,
you, with *les cuisses écartées, les minous affamés,*
you, nuns without lies, without shame, without *culottes*,
your *sacrés culs au* Sacré Coeur,
Who will be your poet? Who will sing your debaucheries?
      O mes petites chiennes lubriques, mes gonzesses,
Mes divines allumeuses, mes salopes, mes coquines,
Mes jolies métisses en rut, très connues dans le X,
J'aime les doux parfums de tes intimités.
J'aime tes petites culottes pleines de mouille.
Plus tes poses sont cochonnes, plus ça m'excite.
      So I come to sing specifically of you —
ravissante jeune femme de l'océan Arctique —
your white skirt hoisted to reveal a *fulgurant* refulgence,
you who adore *un gros braquemart noir*
dans ton petit cul brun,
you who love to dribble *par tous les trous,*
you who treasure *les démolitions anales.*
Ah, my darling forty kilos of perversity,
cupidic image of Tia Bella,
avec ses cheveux châtains, ses yeux noisettes,
je veux enfoncer ma bite jusqu'au fond de ta chatte!

Seduction

à la manière de Bob Dylan

That lamp floating by was a woman's face,
And you do remember, you do remember,
Her sonnets were nettles, how they stung,
How at you she flung tarantula tentacles.

You kissed like you were screaming, "Fire!"
Twinned tongues streamed like kerosene.
Clenched like Professor Humbert & Lolita,
You grappled and drowned in hot wetness.

You were so certain you two could equal
The XXX conversation of the Great Poets
In blues oozed by broke-necked singers,
But she was too much like you, to like you.

A horse, black, charges, searing as scripture,
Through snow: Augean cock plunging into
Stygian — or Sisyphian — pussy, sapping.
Ink copulates with *Intellect*; *Poetry* cries out.

Canticles

1: Rambunctious

Though drab, chill rain infiltrates marrow-deep in April,
I feel like taking her hard in the grass —
To feel a double wetness and softness
Against hardness, a painful pleasure.

2: September 1, 19__

      Awakening early, another morning,
after a night splurged away in phrases,
her wild hands scratching her arms restlessly,
or swafting over such Pre-Raphaelite skin,
in soft Latinate, *doucement*, of saying,
while stars insisted I was forgetting
that instructive dream of desire,
all the time wanting, undiscovering
(for how much longer?), how to escalate
from conjecture to ejaculate joy.

3: Pharisaic Queries

What's cool and wet and heats like fire?
What's tight, then slippery, then tight?
What's hard and soft and long and short?
What's up and down and in and out?

Lust Tussle

à la manière de Darius James

I want any young girl who does everything —
All the devious things a *diva* should do.

Lavishly filthyish, drastically gymnastic,
A jolting, pretty lightning bolt of a girl.

Let her tumble like a star against velvet black,
Her morals crumbling mine all night.

One appealing *belle* sets my bells a-pealing.
I'll melt into her like a second skin.

(Yep, it's important to be verily, extra explicit:
Agèd men doze, young ladies wet dream.)

Let's chase sex, hide an seekin, winkin under sheets.
(All dirt is delicious, if drizzled with honey.)

Watch

That girl with the slithering walk.
Her skin glaring bitter orange: *Cointreau.*

Her panties rustling —
All a-bustle with ass.

Red, moist lips finessing fine, lovely words
Arrange a lavish display, sun-lit.

Little by little, gasps and sighs heat her lips,
Then animated tears, living cries.

Her breasts jousting with her blouse:
Nipples startlingly, vividly rigid.

Inhale her hair's windy April freshness,
While white rum blackens your heart.

What heart?

A Beautiful Plague

To navigate the dark fog of *amour*,
Trace the silver lining of small talk.

Champagne clears away vodka-misted tears.
Her beige chemise better off as cream.

Her speechless kiss precedes her French one.
Feel avid silk, dazzling and bedazzling.

Nymphomania nurses satyriasis:
Fottere, scopare, fregare, et cetera.

When Peeping Tom eyes Sleeping Beauty,
Despair parades through *Paradise.*

Smoke, stench, lust, vomit, booze, slurps, tears.
Then we "Do It Again" …

Despair

Maverick among mares, stallion among fillies,
And rut and rut and rut.

Pivot thy fat beer belly over fine, pubescent thighs.
Turn that foolish, little girl into a snorting bitch.

Her *rouge* lips mimic a line of fine blood.
Her white legs part like her scarlet lips.

You may hold your beloved almost like a lover.
Once you're finished, the sun can very well die.

Darkness must always envelope light, eh?
Every actual night gotta be lived in the dark.

Gynography

Only the dream of Africadia is written here.
District after district, sunflowers glisten.

Some of them are girls.
(Choose the darkest ones for lovers.)

Among all the beautiful girls down here,
Only that one from *Whylah Falls* is beautiful.

Almost un-Nova Scotian, she is so-so-so spectacular:
Moorish-Romany, Indo-Gypsy, mocha-black Mi'kmaq.

A cinnamon-copper Negro with licorice hair:
Bright, Byzantine nobility amid cornfields.

Does a triumphant *négritude* demand solitude?

Bull-headed Minotaur, bellow and moan!

T'ief vocabulary from pulpit and parties.
Go a-courtin with luscious, crushin lips.

Post-Prandial

May I be repeated in your mouth,
O, lover?

Gasps of brandy, sighs of bread:
Silk sheets host Mardi Gras, Easter, and Christmas.

Eyes of candied ginger, as gold as *Calvados*,
Beautiful eyes over beautiful martinis ...

Let kisses founder upon lips:
The ocean founders upon the shore.

Coming first, fine wine refines our swinish finishing:
To sport and joust, refreshed.

And so we perish, breath by exhausting breath —
With Olympic sex, games of lust, gold-medal spirits.

Girl

I

In the living room, where the sun was dying, that Hitchcock blonde —
Poignantly poised — like ice awaiting fire —

Blanched white under her Canaan of yellow hair
(Sultry sparks jostling snow).

Fastidiously melancholy, I acted with apt cold —
As if hotly Pushkinesque,

Craving to ply gold lacquer upon her limbs,
To be that brassy sunlight gilding her snow.

Her mouth spat fire while I fibbed into glasses.
At the black zenith, anxiety jingled with laughter.

Her thighs like a feather pillow
Could suffocate or succour me.

Even stoic coitus could rustle lustre, I thought.
In the economy of *Lust*, I was spent.

A plush, bonny platinum blonde
Turns even a fire-eater to ash.

II

"My baby found me where I was standin,
But she left me on my knees."

Her eyes shine with no lesser brightness
Than the stars themselves. Or worse.

Pitching their pebble brilliance,
Stars swing down.

A blues trumpet torches blue velvet cities.
Ain't my girl as chimerical as the Sphinx?

Her snowness names *Desire* —
Its white trumpets like ocean's wintry roar.

Lemme come unto her like Pushkin with lyre,
Wrapped in *Love*'s warmth, wrapped in its bear fur,

Singing her body's blizzard of beauty —
Then chanting delirious ecstasy —

A sudden smoking volcano, *Love*'s lava,
And a molten, melt-down gold stream of hair.

Helpless?

Are you helpless before what you love?
Do you kneel and howl,
cringe, slaver, drool?
Do you mope and lope about on all fours?
Do you whine and crawl?
Do you slobber and sniffle?
Do you dream of suicide,
then homicide?
Are you so helpless?

Shore

Champagne-with-vodka after tons of cheesecake.
A thin phallus of light over dark water.

Conversation among poets
Is duels, not duets.

Some lovers are not amorous or amoral,
Just amorphous, which is worse.

Haven't you gone begging, begging,
For the soft parts of a woman?

The rain is meringue, dingy,
Over the mad, rabid water,

Foaming, mousse. Constellations
Go dizzy.

The light through the pines —
Grey now, a universe of sorrow.

The promiscuously viscous rain —
A light grey mucus over everything.

How much cold can anyone take?
I see my old skin in a new light.

This *fin d'année* is quasi-scuzzy.
Skull-grim gleams snow, dissolving.

Love is not a word
To fuck with.

Bluing Green

à la manière de Miles Davis

"The problem with jazz is miscegenation"?
　　　　Say I want purity, to be a pure black,
Coloured to purge every bit of whiteness
From my innards, my psyche, my senses,
So that, if I failed, a motherfucker could
Smash me in the face with my trumpet,
Or let me fall like a comic book Capone,
Tasting black blood as it floods my mouth,
My throat slashed by another gangster.
Well, I'd be resurrectin that jive spiritual
Just to crucify its stupid ass!
　　　　Don't I crave a cinematic albescence —
Like lightning rum scorching the throat,
Or napalm eating away superficial flesh,
Cannibalizing it down to the clean bone,
Or a high trumpet note as white as cocaine,
A kiss charging like acid through my dick,
Thanks to *une parisienne* as pale as New York,
Her dark hair falling in sheets around her
Like black shadow around an ivory flame,
Her upbeat allure crazying me like crack
As rich as the notes I'm hitting now?

Because jazz sprouts from gutters,
From stew-soiled beds, genital stink,
Operas o' rapes, crotch-scent wetness,
Whorettes with hips like black mares,
Pallid Barbies all high up in the shit,
A philharmonic orchestra of coitus —
Clarinet of cock, sax of cunt, drum of ass —
So that the rum alchemizing my stomach
Emerges as white-gold notes, molten, volcanic,
In the trumpeting air, now brassy, silvery.
        Remember the clean facts:
We pig out on squalor.
We are only as pure
As the blue inside green.

BLACK *Ice*

Le tragique sera dans la couleur noire!
C'est elle que vous chérirez, rejoindrez, mériterez.
— JEAN GENET

Moral Maxims

for Bernadette Dyer

I — Politics

There's no room for *bonhommie*
In a contracting economy.

Never any dogma
Without some stigma.

It is the glory of government
To turn cream into excrement.

II — Sex

Nothing out-stinks
Male sex instincts.

Cool, Bible-quoting constables
Stall their whores in secret stables.

Suspicion is *Love*'s sharp spice,
But *Lust* is tasty as licorice.

III — Art

To sail *Literature*'s *lascive* sea
Is to face cyclones of nausea.

No matter what the aesthetic —
Art serves best as anaesthetic.

If you crave to win the laurel,
Never with your critics quarrel.

Strive to be as incandescent
As Icarus — in his bright descent.

Progressive Descent

for Afua Cooper

I

Eat with the gusto of maggots eating flesh!

It takes dirt to get dirt.

A corpse a day
Keeps the press corps at bay.

2

Millions die —
And so do millionaires.
(But, first, millions die
Supporting millionaires.)

Banks never have your interest at heart.

The charge for flesh is flesh.

3

All praise is foreplay.

The final grace
That is the grave
Sues the disgrace
That is all love.

Love is painful at first; and it is painful at the end.

20th-Century History

Fascism was popular —
But loud-mouthed and bloody.

Social Credit went bankrupt:
Too much funny money.

Socialism promised Heaven,
But who could afford it?

Hail Capitalism *Rex* —
Tyrannous and sordid.

John Fitzgerald Kennedy

1

Consider John Fitzgerald Kennedy's
Dickinsonian death —
the pure poetry
that is feeling
"physically as if the top
of my head were taken off."

2: Dallas Catullus

Rain hemorrhages like a head-shot president
            spilling a brain-matter rainbow
                        over a backseat of flowers.

The Assassination of Malcolm X

à la manière de Clement Virgo

      His right hand shot to his chest
as sixteen shotgun pellets
punched through the lectern,
cutting short his oration.
Full stop.
      But his left hand also rose —
so that its middle finger
got bullet-battered,
just as blood lurched from his goatee.
      He clutched at his heart,
because so many holes
had suddenly thrown wide
hot red spurts.
      His straight body dropped backwards
stiffly, like a prophet's,
and shattered two chairs.
His head thudded the stage floor.
      A desperate disciple felt,
then fingered a small back wound
saturating clothes scarlet.
But the wounds on the front
were expectorating blood
over the wooden theatre stage —
so much now the floor of a lost Senate.

There were ten punctures in his body,
numbering seven in the heart,
two in the thigh,
one in the left ankle.

There were also four grazes —
one on the right knee,
three across the chest.

This fatal math also counts
a 9-mm slug fired from an automatic,
and a sawed-off, double-barrel shotgun
with two expended shells in the chambers;
ten pieces of lead, probably from a shotgun;
two 9-mm slugs from an automatic;
three .32-calibre slugs from a revolver;
six 9-mm casings;
and three .45-calibre Western shell casings.

Anchoring X's jacket
were an empty eyeglass case
and verses from *The Glorious Qur'an*.

What was not detectable was the violent poetry,
violent scripture, this martyrdom leaked —
a sour, righteous condemnation,
perpetually fountaining, brilliant,
from the holes in the orator's chest,
his multiplied mouths.

The Assassination of Malcolm X (II)

Speak, master, speak! Speak, goddamn it!
— A DISCIPLE OF MALCOLM X (CA. 1964)

Dub him Aswad Zorya Alar, "Black star having wings":
He forced us to be beautiful for the first time.

Bullets turn ordinary martyrs into mud.
But he towers over any three-inch-long obit.

Harlem, NY, Sunday, February 21, 1965:
A sanguine masterpiece of shotgun murder.

Due to the black-panther ferocity of his heart,
His baptismal blood poured out relentlessly.

Into gutters and through dirty streets, it plunged.
Eyeballs expanded mid teeth gleam and cigarettes.

The soulful came runnin with mops and buckets
To sop up every drop and lug it home.

Folks witnessed the *Love* and the *Truth* that poured
Blazing from Malcolm's gasping chest.

Sin-chromed, cast-iron hearts turned tinsel embers.
Teardrops coated tenements and drowned out mosques.

The very air got iced and nailed to the ground.
But disciples caught the last light draining from clouds —

Stagolee's blood issuing passionately, voluptuously,
On that Valentine's Day marked with an X.

IX/XI

for John Fraser, who wrote Violence in the Arts *(1974), and was right.*

I

We told ourselves *History* was finished —
The Holocaust just a museum piece now,
Hitler a cartoon Macbeth, Stalin a wax corpse,
Pol Pot a tin-pot version of crackpot Nixon,
And Rwanda made a theme park of machetes.

It was safe, our white-washed world was now safe:
No more pyramids of bones and hair,
No more napalm to charbroil infants,
No more nerve-gassings of "infidels,"
No more land mines to blow off your legs.

We could tune out the grisly technicolour
Of dark peoples' famines, plagues, massacres,
Or watch their cheap apartment blocks dissolve —
Under the editorial resolve of our munitions.
Our omnipotence was our doled-out avarice.

But all omnipotence has a weakness. Ours meant
The clacking of bankers' never-satisfied teeth,
The bullshit of bought-and-sold elections,
The guffaws of hucksters drowning out
The pure, toxic prayers of those who blame us.

II

Out of our blue-blank, Disney-postcard Heaven,
Came *jihad* squads of suave, aerial assassins,
Whose glistening knives of hijacked jet aircraft
Sliced into hundred-storey-high monoliths —
As white and vulnerable as wedding cakes.

It was violence as judgment, violence as *Kitsch*,
Violence as aviation and concrete, violence
As pornography, violence as *X-acto* blades,
Violence as the President hunkered down in
Bunkers, violence as the Pentagon burned.

It was violence as stock market manipulation,
Violence as crucified eagles, violence as maggots,
Violence as stabbed-out eyes, violence as racism,
Violence as information, violence as shopping,
Violence as the Secretary of Defense, cowering.

Computer terminals gone terminally combustible
Ignited an inferno of black-lettered, white paper,
While plummeting concrete sheared off women's feet
In red or black pumps and cut off fathers' heads and left
Torsos bent over steering wheels in crushed SUVs.

Those jets with their hostage passengers slammed into
And toppled our towers — like Hitler taking Paris.
Our infallible towers, teetered, tottered, tumbled,
Crumbled, and crashed down like two Stalinist statues,
They came down like twin *Titanics*, sinking.

It was trauma and *triage*, to be so shocked awake
To *History*'s revolt, its brutal, blazing insurgency.
But do you have a *right* to finish your bagel and coffee?
Do you have a *right* to see your daughter give birth?
Do you have a *right* to exist without suffering?

III

History shook that city that said, "*History* is history."
A Malcolm X prophecy came to fiery, smoking life
In a King Kong apocalypse of planes hitting towers.
Unanswerably *kamikaze*, candidly unappeasable men
Insisted on dissolving citizens in fire and in glass.

Though civilization often okays being blasé,
On its margins, there's suffering, intense suffering,
Gothic outcasts always dreaming up catastrophes,
And sometimes their lobbed fireballs hit home.
No civilization survives without suffering.

Now when we say, "I love New York," sobs may stun.
Such silent subways right after the sabotage, then
Wailing, yes, and instant spirituals — as in so many other
Exploded cities: London, Hiroshima, Baghdad,
And Halifax, Nova Scotia, on December 6, 1917.

Let the damage be remembered, for we are damaged,
The dead given faces, our broadcast dead reclaimed,
The nightmares witnessed, pondered, documented,
The shed blood kept warm and wet and vivid, jetting, jetting,
From real bodies, our own, in pain — raw, ungodly, humanizing pain.

History

for Charles R. Saunders

Against endless, black, forever, dark nothing,
Blanches the blear North Star.

Hot-eyed, I look up, aspiring to warm those stars.
But, cold and uncaring, they just grow colder.

To destroy everything,
A nihilist must be optimistic.

If I had any luck at all,
I'd have some rum.

Depression is boring.
Let tears spring as sprightly as piano notes.

Let us breathe pain with every breath —
Until we fall, breathless.

The plot of life, *Kemosabe*,
Trails off to a grave.

BLACK Cloud

BLACK is an open umbrella.
— GWENDOLYN BROOKS

Jean Chrétien

1: Revised Standard Version

A Frankenstein-masked, meeching, elfish ghoul,
Skulking in a graveyard of prime ministers,
Admiring how they bagged elections —
Or dreading how they later got sacked —
Those lumberjacks hulking in silk suits,
Those attorneys awkward in buckskins,
Defining the country as one more strip mine
After one more lucrative deforestation,
All Chrétien ever wanted was to join
This Gothic junkyard of shat-upon statues,
Clutching the *Criminal Code* in one hand,
A golf club in the other,
While sloshing out rhetoric that was martinis
And pabulum drizzled over cooing ministers.

Slick, he slipped through cracks in bad news
And popped up gleaming like a televangelist,
While acting Laurier with an *Alley Oop*-squint —
"Le p'tit gars" orating, "C'est de la bullshit,"
His speech spitting a pepper-spray clarity.

His Canada was cant and cannot,
A Parliament of lepers and peons,
A politics of nothing doing
Cos doing nothing means nothing's wrong.

He was the perfect mime of a prime minister,
Choosing to ape the mannerisms of the dead,
To shuffle, Zombie-like, into *History*,
Through a labyrinth of funhouse mirrors
Stuttering his forged, misshapen greatness.

2

He was depressive, swinish, foolish, garrulous,
Wrathful, calculating, tricky, ornery, arrogant,
Execrable, difficult, vengeful, professional, sly,
Narrow, bull-headed, deft, lawyerly, egotistical,
Despicable, vital, and he was all of these things
Every single day of every single election year.
Then, he got worse.

Pierre Elliott Trudeau (1919–2000): Elegy

Brooding in his Gothic tower of words,
He is Yeatsian, a chiselled chimera.
Or he's proud, savage Plato in a canoe,
Cast off in a wilderness of cameras.

As black and white as antique film
Or gunpowder, this grainy phantom
Is only mirage and images now —
As dead and immortal as Latin.

No rubes craved to be like him, carved
Out of photo-ops and alabaster,
Cranky, dismissive of alibis,
And as cunning as a pastor.

Lofty, above provincials, he danced,
Never wincing, though we'd bandy
Knives, brooding to play Brutus
To his Caesar, pirouetting, dandy.

Elegy on a Theme by Gasparini

à la manière de Kirk Johnson

       Limb by trellising limb, she hoists herself,
Aspiring up, eyeing stars spiralling shy
The maple's mulling leaves, while vermilion
Roses and lovers' nodding skulls congress,
Squalled in concupiscent conspiracy.
       Breathless, she inhales leaves, their incensed green
Ebony, dark narcotic chlorophyll,
Then faints at the crux of branches and trunk.
Her heart startles to a stop. Paralyzed,
Sepulchred by green foliage — camouflage,
She wanes to crippled limbs, quadriplegic,
Genealogy stripped to bone china,
Delicate with *craquelure*, while squirrel thieves
Ransack her pockets, pillage her ribcage,
Pirate crows abscond with two tinny eyes —
Soft, false jewels–and ants tunnel through her skull.
       But, her body comes clear once October
Gales splay and disintegrate flaking leaves,
And weak flesh has pined away, as it must,
And a lover, squinting into starlight,
Spies, instead, a sour, osseous moon glaring
Maliciously from skeletal tangles.

Elegy for Blair States (1959–2001)

He has gone far from his name.
It is now like so much foam
Stranded, fading, on a beach —
When the wave undoes its stitch
And unravels again to sea.

He is now no more an "I."
His bright, ebullient being —
Blond-brash as bullion — was song
Not muted by mortal flesh,
But fire incapable of ash.

His name was an ex-slave name,
Remembering where we're from
("States," some drunk British clerk quipped
For slaves from the "U.S." crept.)

Now, he's fully free, escaped —
Like tidal shapes oceans sculpt.

BLACK *Light*

It wasn't a blackness that absorbed light;
it was a blackness that displaced it ...
— JEAN AVELINE

A Discourse on My Name

First, it is thoroughly British:
George is English, *Elliott* Scottish, and *Clarke* Irish.
Of course, this fact makes it a misnomer,
For I am an Africadian —
A Black Nova Scotian of African-American
And Mi'kmaq roots,
A descendant of slaves and encircled First Nations,
Peoples bossed and bartered by the British.
Being so objectively Anglophone,
My name is either evidence
Of *our* utter subjection —
Or it exacts a most curious revenge.

I do like that *George* descends from the Greek for *farmer*,
And, though I've never farmed,
I enjoy my uncultivated acreage in Three Mile Plains
And my feral garden, part weeds, part roses,
Part onions, garlic, raspberries, lilac,
In Toronto, "the meeting place."
Elliott is Jewish: it derives from Hebrew
For *Man of God*,
And though I am amongst the bleakest, blackest sinners,
Perhaps this naming explains
My constant admiration of virtue,
My constant desire for redemption.

Clarke echoes Old English for *religious man*,
But French for a *scholar*,
And so, as a doctorated esquire —
Ph.D., LLD (Hon.), D.Litt (Hon.), D.Litt (Hon.) —
Who owns land near the Windsor Plains African Baptist Church,
I can swing between being a cleric
And a clerk —
When ah ain't farmin.

My mother selected my first two names.
But her choice of *George*
Had nothing to do with George VI, George Washington,
George Washington Carver, Gorgeous George,
George of the Jungle, Curious George,
Or even "Georgie Porgie,
Puddin an pie,
Who kissed the girls
And made em sigh."
No, she named me after her father's father,
George Johnson,
A Mi'kmaq still living when I was born,
Who wanted a new boy to carry on his name,
After the previous recipient,
His first-born grandson,
George Albert Hamilton,
Born in December 1925,
Died with a rope around his neck
In Fredericton, New Brunswick, in July 1949,
When my mother was ten,
And I was still a decade away from conception.

As for *Elliott*, it got naught to do with literature!
Folks imagine I's named for Miss George Eliot,
But the truth be more poetic!
While pregnant with me,
Through the summer and fall of 1959,
As John F. Kennedy was stealing his steely way
Toward the White House,
My mother was watching black-and-white television,
The primitive, classic "box,"
And, especially, the crime show, *The Untouchables*,
Starring dour Robert Stack as indefatigable Elliott Ness,
Whose name she rightly pinched.
Thus, my "writerly" cognomen is really
Proof of my television-besotted origins,
And it explains why folks prefer to hear me read poetry aloud,
Rather than read it silently themselves:
There's a bit of a ham in me.

Clarke is the title of woe,
The site of my bondage to African slavery
In its Caribbean phase.
My father inherited this brand from a sailor,
Called either "Morris" or "Norris,"
Who came either from Barbados or Jamaica,
And who washed ashore in Halifax, N.S.,
During the Great Depression,
Just long enough to marry my father's mother
And produce my father,
Then promptly vamoose and vanish.
Part of me is thus proudly West Indian,

Probably Bajan
(I like the potential connection to Austin Clarke,
The Bajan-Can novelist, not the Irish poet).
But I feel that *Clarke* is too much a part of clanking history —
Anchors, chains, leg-irons, fetters, horseshoes —
To be borne easily,
Particularly when my Carib forebear didn't care
To see his name take root in Canada,
This "collection of huts,"
But bore away upon the seven seas.

But I likely get my wanderlust from him,
From Morris/Norris Clarke,
As much as I get my love of our land from my mother
(*née* Johnson),
My love of books from my autodidact father.

To honour my parents,
I keep this name, these names,
All their bloody antiquity intact.

⋄·

Names are never simple things, eh?
They hold something of *Fate*.

Autobiography (II)

I look at myself, unforgiven, forgotten,
A forty-something, heartless simpleton,
A buck-toothed, loud-laughing, so-called poet:
Ink on my hands like bomb residue.

Mortality Sonnet

How the columns of the body
Corrode and collapse,
Despite girdings of cotton and silk,
Or buttresses of expensive ointments.

How *Death* camps out in the body
To seize it by surprise.

How it charges, then, through veins
And arteries, or along nerves and muscle,
Discharging tissue and organs,
So that the heart calcifies to bone.

The issue is to sing until breath is gone.

Flagging, I hurl these words
To shout down *Time*
Just as it becomes *Eternity.*

Ending

All things must pass;
      Even *Pain* dwindles like sun-singed water:
Dew refreshes grass
      Cattle crush *en route* to slaughter.

               ·◊·

Culture is what you eat; *Nature* is what eats you.

               ·◊·

Laughter from the funeral home:
      An axe of light maims the dark.

               ·◊·

Relax: you only hit rock bottom once you're buried.

BLACK *Velvet*

Is it blacker? Was it blacker?
—— EZRA POUND

Decima

for Makeda Silvera

Nearing midnight, the clock slows down,
So I can compose this strange poem
Dependent on eight-syllable
Lines stacked in a bundle of ten,
So eighty bits of speech cohere
In communicating chaos.
I'm getting there though, as the clock
Clucks down the long sixty seconds,
And the poem takes shape, painfully,
While ink screws down contours of thought.

À Geeta

Call yourself, glancingly,
"A small, brown woman,"
for the phrase is exact.
You are diminutive, Indian, and *une femme,*   .
An expert in xviii-century French erotica —
All that revolutionary Romanticism,
The pillow talk of *philosophes,*
Setting Crébillon against and over Diderot,
For you prefer common-sense cotton to slinky silk,
And value sassy erudition over easy seduction.

       True: you stand just five feet tall,
 But your mind encompasses God
And your heart compasses the world,
And you overwhelm even towering fools.

       Say you're pure-blooded, a Brahmin,
A Hindu whose eyes glorify Africa, cradle of light,
And whose skin is alive with night-undressing sun:
That would be truth too.

       Ah, Pomona of Mauritius,
Kali of Île Maurice —
Honey surges in all your body's canals,
Plies gold-leaf liqueur upon your limbs,
Sears henna into your eyes,
Becomes copper igniting velvet night,
And bronzes you, spiting Canada's white desert.

To embrace you is to embrace *colour* —
Pungent spice, piquant speechifying —
And raise sari arias of cinnamon and cayenne.
        Are you talkative? A chatterbox? Yes?
Well, consider the gourmet meal
Your voluptuous lips make of words.
Even your English errors are erotic!
Remember the time you called the hotel
And told the switchboard operator,
"I want to sleep with —
I mean, speak to —
The guest in room 61"?
And though you scan Cixous, *sans souci*,
The only travel writing you admire
Is restaurant reviews —
For you sip those *Godiva* chocolates
That I, swinish, gobble,
While your indulgence of distant India
Adheres to a glowing scripture of curry.
        I have roamed with you along beaches —
In North Carolina, Barbados, and Mauritius —
Plastered by the foam-stucco'd sea,
While sun splintered through palm fronds,
And some crimson bird-of-paradise erupted
From amid slippery greenery,

And your dress sometimes was just a breeze,
Or the look of moonlight after rain,
Or the green scent of the wind —
The liberty of the Mauritian Republic,
While your tutoring tongue
Lectured away libertinage,
Erasing my unspeakable lies
With enviable truth.

      O wife, so tawny, never naughty,
Excepting the verve of your eyes —
Or the lick of *brio* on your tongue —
To hold you like the ocean holds the sun,
That is love —
And you must be clasped as closely
As a country no one has colonized.
      "A small, brown woman"?
No.
You are a fifth element, feelings, and an epoch.

Will

I

I would like, if possible,
An oasis beside the Atlantic,
A round, stone tower
Encircled by sunflowers,
And, of course, an apple tree or two,
And lilies (white) and lilacs (violet),
Also, a stone bench for lovers
For those sudden Nova Scotian springs,
Sodden with perfumes and profuse with sun,
Inspiring volumes of blackberries in August.
Indoors, I must needs have a marble bathtub,
Big enough for two,
And a small library with only unforgettable books,
Including one by Sappho and that one by Ruggles
("died Novascotia 1788 and a tory"),
And *Cane*, *The Cantos*, and The Canticles
(I would be selective).
And I will drain jugs of Grand Pré wine,
Along with much *Fernandes Black Label* rum
And *Barbancourt* white rum,
Feast on miracles of fish and bread,
And I will sit in the *soleil* of April
For thirty, gorgeous, too-brief days,
And I will sit in its shadow the other 335 days,
Until beauty can flower again.

I will see in black scarves,
A reverence for independence,
And in whatever painting done on the wall,
A door may be cut through,
Interrupting representations of intemperate rum-drinking —
So be it! —
Or of a black Christ, sunlit, ascending, ascending.
And I will spend my days worshipping Sappho
And Sheba.

II

For my funeral, here's what I'd like:
A copper or bronze casket, please,
And wash my body thoroughly
And wrap me in pristine white linen
(No suit!),
And set my head on the pillow
My mother made for me
When I was still a little boy,
And flowers should be wildflowers
And sunflowers, roses, lilies.
Let the service be held
At Cornwallis Street United Baptist Church
(That African Baptist church, est. 1832),
Where my great-granddaddy preached.

I pray my daughter, Aurélia, will forgive me,
Though I was a long-distance father,
And I pray my wife will forgive me,
Though I was a vain and selfish husband.
Let there be music — lots, *lots!*
Rev. Larry Croxen on sanctified guitar,
And Four the Moment's holy songs
And the choir doing "Pass Me Not"
Mournful, *mournful!*
Also Gilly Daye testifying to the blues.
Let poetry be read,
Including verses from the Song of Solomon
And Pound's "The River Merchant's Wife: A Letter"
(because it awakened me to poetry),
then my own version,
"The River Pilgrim: A Letter."
Burial must be at Maplewood Cemetery,
In Windsor, Nova Scotia,
Right beside my mother,
And someone, please, plant Lombardy poplars nearby.

BLACK Mail

L'ombre et la lumière emmêlent leurs palettes …
— CALIXTHE BEYALA

"Black Power": My dream name — "X. States" — is cannily chosen.
I cannot recover an original African genealogy, but my maternal roots
lay in the Chesapeake Bay region of *dem* United States, whence my
matrilineal ancestors, liberated by British troops during the War of 1812,
got shipped to Nova Scotia, along with 2,000 other ex-US ex-slaves.
You see where I'm going — or coming from — with this? I am "ex"
the "States," and that noun is also a uniquely African-Nova Scotian
(Africadian) surname, signifying where most of us are/were from …
(But may I also signal here my partial *Mi'kmaq* Nationhood?)

"Coda: George & Rue" refers to the actual hangings of George and
Rufus Hamilton, in Fredericton, New Brunswick, in July 1949, for
having bludgeoned a taxi driver to death, with a hammer, the previous
January. Curiously, they came from a Black community near Windsor,
Nova Scotia, where, during slavery, a black boy was slain by a blow
from a hammer wielded by his master. Cf. *Execution Poems* (2001) and
George & Rue (2005).

"IV. i": *Priminery* is archaic English for *difficulty*; *crepuscolari* ("Twilight poets") is the brand name of Italian Laforguians.

"IV. iii": In 1998, U.S. President William Jefferson Clinton III told a prosecutor, in testimony, "It depends on what the meaning of the word 'is' is."

"À Arthur Nortje": The South African poet (1942–70) committed suicide in Oxford, England, after an abortive emigration to Canada (1967–70).

"Au Tombeau de Pound (II)": Cf. "Au Tombeau de Pound" in *Blue* (2001).

"Sermon on J.W. Doull's Used Books Store": His shop's in Halifax, NS. The Trudeau epigraph is from *Mémoires politiques* (1993).

"VI. i": Cf. "I. v" in *Blue* (2001).

"Africadian Experience": "1917" refers to the Halifax Explosion of December 6, 1917, that rendered Halifax, NS, a preview of the A-bombing of Hiroshima, Japan, on August 6, 1945. These sightings recur in "IX/XI."

"La Vérité à Ottawa (II)": The *Secret Bench of Knowledge*, a sculpture by Lea Vivot, does sit before the Bibliothèque Nationale, rue Wellington, in Ottawa, and it does carry the inscription I quote. Later in the poem, spy, hear, a reference to Sade — that is to say, Sade [shar-day] Adu, the Anglo-Nigerian pop vocalist.

"Bluing Green": The poem riffs on "Blue in Green," a Miles Davis masterpiece from his album, *Kind of Blue* (1959). But it is also informed by Davis's as-told-to-Quincy Troupe *Autobiography* (1985).

"John Fitzgerald Kennedy — 1": The quotation is from the prescient Emily Dickinson (1830–86).

"The Assassination of Malcolm X": The poem mines forensic reports on the grisly martyrdom of El-Hajj Malik El-Shabazz (b. 1926) on Sunday, February 21, 1965.

"The Assassination of Malcolm X (II)": "Stagolee" is the archetypal, semi-legendary, African-American "bad man" — not to be messed with!

"History": "Kemosabe" is a faux "Indian" word, invented by Hollywood. It means "friend."

Jean Chrétien : *Oui, il a dit, "C'est de la bullshit!"* October 21, 2003.

"Elegy on a Theme by Gasparini" responds to Leonard Gasparini's fine poem about the discovery of a woman's clothed remains in a tree in a Toronto park in 1975. Find his "Elegy" in his *Selected Poems* (Toronto: Hounslow, 1993). My style is indebted, however, to the works of my poet-cousin, Kirk Johnson (1973–).

"Decima": This verse form is written as indicated within the poem.

Note: The poems titled numerically, "IV. i" — "VII," conclude the "Blue Elegies" introduced in *Blue* (2001).

BLACK *Magic*

Noire de mes rêves …
— CALIXTHE BEYALA

The *innocent* readers were Paul Zemokhol, Silas White, Andrew Steeves, Evie Shockley, Simone Poirier-Bures, Leilah Nadir, David Kellogg, Gary Geddes, John Fraser, and Sandra Barry. Geeta Paray-Clarke *is* uncorrupted beauty. The sins herein are all mine.

Black flared up out of Durham (US), Barcelona (Spain), Bellagio (Italy), Sliema (Malta), and Monte Carlo (Monaco), and Halifax, Montreal, Ottawa, Toronto, and Banff, 1994–2005. (It was *Blue*, first.)

Thanks to the Rockefeller Foundation of New York City, the McGill Institute for the Study of Canada, and the Banff Centre for the Arts for the time required to cantilever, gerrymander, and engineer, these poems. I am also grateful for my patrons: Victoria University/University of Toronto, Dr. Sonia Labatt, and the Pierre Elliott Trudeau Foundation of Montreal.

Some of these inklings debuted in *The Dalhousie Review; To Find Us: Words and Images of Halifax* [Halifax]; *Shunpiking; The Gaspereau Review; Vallum; Kola; Headlight* [Concordia University]; *Poetry Canada Review; Murderous Signs; ARC; 25 Years of Tree: The Tree Reading Series 25th Anniversary Anthology* [Ottawa]; *Perceptions 2003* [University of Toronto]; *Ex Libris* [Trinity College, University of Toronto]; *Acta Victoriana* [Victoria University, University of Toronto]; *Exile; The Toronto Star; The Walrus; Variety Crossing — 6th Volume; Canada Watch; The New Quarterly; Lichen; Cantos Cadre; Windsor Review; Prairie Fire; ARIEL; Event; Canadian Literature; Prism; and Geist;* in the US, in *Dialog* [Duke University]; *Near South;* and in *Poetry International;* and in England in *Dance the Guns to Silence: 100 Poems for Ken Saro-Wiwa.* Other poems first appeared in these limited editions: *Running with Scissors* [*Blue (II)*] (Montreal, QC: Cumulus Press, 2001); and *Africadian History* (Kentville, NS: Gaspereau Press, 2001). Two poems first aired on Canadian Broadcasting Corporation radio: "IX/XI" (2002) and "Mortality Sonnet" (2003). Flowers to the editors, hosts, and publishers.

Black was typeset in 10 pt. Bembo on a 15 pt. leading. It was designed and typeset by Teresa Bubela. The photo credits belong to Anonymous (p. 47); Author (pp. 27, 56, 58, 62, 95); Donna Barry (p. 141); presspics@gmail.com (p. 61); Candidate [*John Fitzgerald Kennedy, Minneapolis, 1960*] © *John Fraser (p. 104); Public Archives of New Brunswick (pp. 39, 69); Le Roi Ray (p. 151); National Library of Canada (p. 75); and Ricardo Scipio (pp. 10, 30, 52, 76, 88, 96, 114, 122, 132).*

BLACK *Beauty*

Nigra sum, sed formosa.
— CANTICUM CANTICORUM

THE JOURNAL OF THE BARBADOS MUSEUM AND
HISTORICAL SOCIETY: PUPILS OF THE CHARTERHOUSE

CLARKE, GEORGE ELLIOTT, (June 1824–1828 or 9). b. July 14, 1811.
1st son of Forster Clarke (d.1840) of Barbados
and his wife Hannah Prescod.
Trinity College, Cambridge, B.A. 1831. Entered Middle Temple 1833.
Called to the Bar, 1836.
Clarke owned Stepney Plantation, parish of St. George, Barbados.
Died at Frampost, East Grinstead, Sussex, 22 Feb. 1877. See M.I. on brass
in St. George's Parish Church, Barbados, erected by his daughter.
The tomb of Clarke is neatly executed in white marble on a black slab.

THE JOURNAL OF CANADIAN EX-SLAVE HISTORY: SURVIVORS

GEORGE ELLIOTT CLARKE is a native of Three Mile Plains, Nova Scotia, born on February 12, 1960. A poet, his critically acclaimed and popular titles include *Whylah Falls* (1990), *Beatrice Chancy* (1999), *Execution Poems* (2001), *Blue* (2001), and *Illuminated Verses* (2005). His staged opera libretti are *Beatrice Chancy* (1998) and *Québécité* (2003). His debut novel is *George & Rue* (2005). A recipient of the Archibald Lampman Award (1991), the Portia White Prize (1998), The Governor-General's Award for Poetry (2001), the Martin Luther King, Jr. Achievement Award (2004), and the Pierre Elliott Trudeau Fellowship Prize (2005), Clarke is the inaugural E.J. Pratt Professor of Canadian Literature at the University of Toronto. He lives in Toronto, owns land in Nova Scotia.